AF097303

Dedicated To:
Brooklyn

Written By: Abigail Gartland

Hello, my name is St. Maria Goretti!

I was born in Italy in 1890!

From the time I was a very little girl, I loved Jesus very much.

I spent a lot of my time praying with my family.

One day, I was doing some work around my house with my little sister.

A young man walked right into my house, and he was very mad

was very afraid, but I knew that God was with me.

The man was very mean to me and hurt me badly.

Even though what the man did was wrong, I forgave him.

After I forgave him, I joined Jesus and Mary in Heaven.

I pray for you every day.

Have you ever had a chance to forgive someone?

Forgiveness means to say "it's okay" when someone does something to hurt you.

When has someone forgiven you?

You ask forgiveness when you say you are sorry for hurting someone else.

Jesus forgives us when we say we are sorry.

You can celebrate my feast day with me on July 6th!

I pray for you every day of your life.

St. Maria Goretti, Pray for Us

Copyright:

Clipart: © PentoolPixie © LimeandKiwiDesigns
Licensed purchased: 1/10/2024

About the Author

Abigail Gartland

I love the saints and I love my faith. The idea for sharing the stories of the saints with little ones came when my dear friends were expecting their first baby. I wanted to create something as unique and special as our friendship. Each book is dedicated to very special people and groups who have enriched my faith in different ways. I am blessed to write these stories and appreciate the unending support of my family and friends. When I am not writing, I am a middle school teacher. I hope you enjoy these stories. I pray for each and every person who opens one of my books to learn more about the saints.

Abbie

www.ingramcontent.com/pod-product-compliance
Lightning Source LLC
LaVergne TN
LVHW061633070526
838199LV00071B/6661